1620

Submarine—
Cornelius Drebbel

Karl Drais

1655

Self-propelled
wheelchair—
Stephen Farffler

1830

Intercity passenger
train—
George Stephenson

1733

Baby carriage—
William Kent

1852

Safety elevator—
Elisha Otis

1760

Roller skates—
John Joseph Merlin

1852

Steam-powered
airship—
Henri Giffard

1769

Steam-powered
land vehicle—
Nicolas-Joseph Cugnot

1863

Subway—
London Underground

1783

Hot-air balloon—
*Joseph and
Étienne Montgolfier*

1869

Rickshaw—
Jonathan Goble

1787

Steamboat—
John Fitch

1880

Improved life raft—
Maria Beasley

1803

Steam locomotive—
Richard Trevithick

1807

Hydrogen-powered
vehicle—
François Isaac de Rivaz

1885

Gasoline-powered
motorcycle—
Gottlieb Daimler

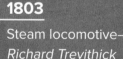

to There

INVENTIONS THAT CHANGED THE WAY THE WORLD MOVES

By Vivian Kirkfield

Illustrated by Gilbert Ford

Houghton Mifflin Harcourt

Boston New York

*To Josh, Emily, Jeremy, and Sophie . . . Like the visionaries
in this book, I hope you will follow your dreams, because nothing is
impossible if you can imagine it.*
–V.K.

To Drew, who's always designing a better system
–G.F.

Text copyright © 2021 by Vivian Kirkfield
Illustrations copyright © 2021 by Gilbert Ford

hmhbooks.com

The illustrations in this book were painted in traditional watercolors and finished digitally in Photoshop and Illustrator.
The text type was set in Century Schoolbook.
The display type was set in Proxima Nova and Archer.

Library of Congress Cataloging-in-Publication Data
Names: Kirkfield, Vivian, author. | Ford, Gilbert, author. Title: From here to there : inventions that changed the way
the world moves / Vivian Kirkfield, Gilbert Ford. | Description: Boston : Houghton Mifflin Harcourt, 2021. | Includes
bibliographical references. | Audience: Ages 7 to 10 | Audience: Grades 2–3 | Summary: "Celebrating the invention of
vehicles, this collective biography tells the inspiring stories of the visionaries who changed the way we move through
air, water, and land. Perfect for fans of Mistakes that Worked and Girls Think of Everything." —Provided by publisher
Identifiers: LCCN 2019043076 (print) | LCCN 2019043077 (ebook) | ISBN 9781328560919 (hardcover) | ISBN
9780358359067 (ebook) | Subjects: LCSH: Transportation—Biography—Juvenile literature. | Classification: LCC HE151.4
.K57 2021 (print) | LCC HE151.4 (ebook) | DDC 629.04/60922—dc23
LC record available at https://lccn.loc.gov/2019043076
LC ebook record available at https://lccn.loc.gov/2019043077

Manufactured in China
SCP 10 9 8 7 6 5 4 3 2 1
4500805631

Bibliography Photo Credits:
Chapter Four — First gas-powered automobile photo: www.daimler.com/company/tradition/
company-history/1885-1886.html | Chapter Five — Eric Wickman Hupmobile photo: www.
startribune.com/greyhound-the-puppy-years/279683102 | Chapter Six — Goddard and rocket
photo: www.nasa.gov/centers/goddard/about/history/dr_goddard.htm

Contents

Introduction

"Are we there yet?" Whether it's reaching a family vacation destination or shopping for a new pair of shoes, we all want to get where we are going as quickly as we can.

These days, we move around by car and bus, train and plane, bike and skateboard and scooter. And new ways are being developed to help us move faster, farther, and more efficiently. Self-driving vehicles and space flights into the stratosphere are realities.

Yet once upon a time, the only way to move from place to place was to walk or run or be carried by another person. Then someone made friends with a wild horse—or ox, or mastodon—and jumped on its back. But it wasn't until the invention of the wheel that things really got rolling.

Without the wheel, there would be no bicycle. And without the bicycle, there would be no car, motorcycle, or even airplane.

So who were the people who came up with better, faster, more efficient ways to move over land, sea, and air? They were visionaries who experimented, failed, and tried again and again until they invented things that changed the way the world moves.

Life is like riding a bicycle. To keep your balance, you must keep moving.

— Albert Einstein

Chapter One

Boys Who Dream of Flying

Joseph and Étienne Montgolfier and Manned Balloon Flight

t a time when most of the world believed human flight was impossible, one boy thought differently.

When Joseph Montgolfier gazed out the window at school, his teachers told him to stop dreaming. Why couldn't he pay attention like his brother Étienne? But Joseph *was* paying attention—to a bird soaring in the sky. Joseph was wondering if he could fly too.

Born in 1740 in Annonay, France, Joseph had fifteen brothers and sisters. He was best friends with only one of them—his youngest brother, Étienne. Étienne spoke eloquently, dressed elegantly, and had a good head for business. Joseph was the exact opposite. But the brothers shared a love of science.

France

Étienne

Joseph

One cold November day in 1782, Joseph watched cinders dance in the fireplace. They floated up the chimney. Joseph wondered if soldiers could be lifted into the air and transported to a battlefield using the same force that lifted the cinders.

Grabbing sticks and string, Joseph built a small A-frame. He covered it with thin fabric. Then he twisted papers, lit them on fire, and pushed the tiny torches under the little tent.

Whoosh! Up it floated, until it bumped into the ceiling!

Joseph raced to show his brother the floating tent.

Together, Joseph and Étienne built a larger model of the experiment: a big ball made of paper and covered with silk.

In a meadow, they secured the balloon with ropes. They lit a fire under it.

Whoosh! The ropes broke. The balloon shot up. It sailed over the trees. Joseph and Étienne couldn't wait to build an even bigger balloon.

They made calculations, drew diagrams, and gathered supplies. Fabric filled every room as they measured and cut. Thread littered the hallways as they sewed. Two thousand buttons sparkled and shone as friends and family fastened them with needle and thread to connect the segments of the balloon.

Finally, the balloon was ready. This time, Joseph and Étienne built a bonfire in the center of town.

Joseph believed that a mysterious gas in the smoke, which he called Montgolfier gas, lifted the balloon. He thought that if the smoke was dark, thick, and smelly, the balloon would go higher, so he added damp straw and shredded wool to the flames. He didn't realize that the balloon rose because the heated molecules of air in the balloon spread out and were less dense and lighter than the cooler air outside the balloon. *Molécules*, or "minute particles" in French, were discussed by Daniel Bernoulli in *Hydrodynamica*, published in 1738. Bernoulli said that gases consist of great numbers of molecules moving in all directions and heat is simply the energy created by their motion.

"*Lachez tout!*" Étienne shouted. "Let go!"

Whoosh! The balloon shot up. It floated across a field. The brothers chased after it. The towns-people chased after the brothers. And by the time they found the balloon more than a mile away, Joseph and Étienne were already planning their next demonstration.

Not every launch was successful. Some of the balloons burned up. Many failed to lift off because of bad weather conditions. Still, the Montgolfier brothers never stopped trying.

Word spread to King Louis XVI. He summoned the brothers. But Joseph did not like speaking in front of people and would not go. Though Étienne didn't know if he could make the balloon fly with-out Joseph, he knew he had to try.

On a sunny September day in 1783, in front of the palace at Versailles, Étienne built a fire, adding old boots and rotten meat to it. The smoke was thicker, darker, and smellier than ever. The king watched from his balcony as into a woven wicker cage stepped . . .

Building huge balloons costs a lot of money. Fortunately, the Montgolfiers' father owned a successful paper factory, and he promised to fund their experiments—on the condition that they promise never to go up in one of their balloons if it was untethered.

. . . a duck, a rooster, and a sheep.

Eyes watered.

Noses wrinkled.

People retched.

Whoosh! Wide-eyed, the crowd watched as the menagerie ascended into the sky, over the palace spires, and out of sight.

Members of the Academy of Science recovered the balloon. The animals were unharmed. The king was impressed. But he had a new challenge for the brothers: Could they build a balloon that would carry a *person* into the air?

Étienne told the king they could build a balloon that would carry *two!*

The king originally wanted to send condemned criminals up in the balloon in case of mishap. But Jean-François Pilâtre de Rozier, a science teacher, and Marquis François d'Arlandes, a soldier, appealed to the king. They felt that the honor of being the first person to soar into the air should not go to someone who had broken the law. The king agreed.

Pilâtre de Rozier   François d'Arlandes

Étienne and Joseph worked day and
night. It wasn't long before the new balloon was
bigger than a house.

On November 21, 1783, in Paris, a blazing fire roared in an
iron furnace. Two brave men stepped into a basket beneath an
enormous tent of fabric.

The balloon tugged at the ropes.

Fear tugged at Étienne's heart.

What if it rained? What if there was too much wind?

What if the aeronauts got hurt?

Étienne could wait no longer.

He cut the ropes!

Whoosh! The balloon rose.

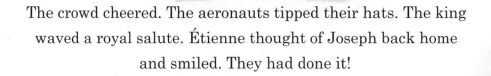

The crowd cheered. The aeronauts tipped their hats. The king
waved a royal salute. Étienne thought of Joseph back home
and smiled. They had done it!

For the next two hundred years, scientists and inventors developed aircraft that flew higher and higher, faster and faster, until finally, on July 20, 1969, men walked on the moon. And it all started with Joseph and Étienne Montgolfier, two brothers, as different as could be, who worked together to take the first step in that starry direction.

Benjamin Franklin, who happened to be in France to negotiate the Treaty of Paris between the United States and England after the American Revolution, watched that first manned hot-air balloon flight. He wrote in his journal, "We observed it lift off in the most majestic manner. When it reached around 250 feet in altitude, the intrepid voyagers lowered their hats to salute the spectators. We could not help feeling a certain mixture of awe and admiration."

Chapter Two

With His Own Two Feet

Karl Drais Invents the Bicycle

Boom! In 1815, a volcano in Indonesia erupted. Ash circled the globe. Seasons shifted. The next summer, snow fell in Germany. Oats withered. Horses starved. Trains, cars, and buses had not been invented yet, so without a horse to ride, Karl Drais had only his own two feet to get where he needed to go.

When Mt. Tambora erupted, fifty-five million tons of sulfur dioxide gas rose more than twenty miles into the air and combined with millions of tons of ash to form sulfuric acid, creating strange weather conditions in many parts of the world. In New England, farmers who lost crops headed west, hoping for a better life. And while vacationing in Switzerland, a group of friends challenged one another to see who could write the scariest story while they stayed indoors due to the cold and rainy weather. Eighteen-year-old Mary Shelley thus began writing *Frankenstein,* considered by many to be the first science-fiction novel ever written.

Karl remembered skating on icy lakes when he was a boy, flying like the wind. Left foot—push! Right foot—push! Steady, steady, balance! If only he could move like that along unfrozen ground.

Born in Karlsruhe, Germany, in 1785, Karl Drais studied to be a forest ranger, but what he loved most of all was tinkering in his workshop. He invented a hand-operated railcar that is still in use today.

Germany

Berlin

Karlsruhe

Munich

Determined to build a vehicle that he could propel with his own two feet, Karl tinkered in his workshop.

He measured and mitered. Sawed and sanded. Heated and hammered.

The first vehicle he constructed had four wheels. It was heavy and cumbersome—one person could not make it move.

Karl took off two wheels. He fashioned handlebars. He attached a seat covered with leather. People passed his workshop wondering what crazy contraption he was building. But Karl paid no attention.

He measured and mitered. Sawed and sanded. Heated and hammered.

On June 12, 1817, Karl tested his invention. He called it a *Laufmaschine,* which means "running machine" in German. Sitting on the seat, he powered it by pushing his feet against the ground. When the machine picked up speed, Karl lifted his feet and coasted along.

Left foot—push! Right foot—push! Steady, steady, balance!

An eight-mile journey took only an hour. Without the machine, it would have taken more than three. Karl was onto something big. Back at his workshop, he added a string brake for slowing and stopping, an umbrella in case it rained, and a sail that could be unfurled to take advantage of wind power.

Within a month, newspapers announced that Karl would ride his running machine thirty-one miles from Karlsruhe to Kehl.

He set off one day at noon.

Men stopped. Women stared. Children cheered.

Karl's leather-booted feet propelled the *Laufmaschine* faster and faster.

Left foot—push! Right foot—push! Steady, steady, balance!

Even though his heart raced and his feet felt as if they were on fire, Karl pressed on. At four p.m., local officials at Kehl confirmed that Karl Drais had arrived. No one had ever traveled that far in so little time on a self-propelled vehicle. Karl's *Laufmaschine* may not have been perfect, but you can't stop a great idea.

Karl's running machine had many problems. It cost forty guilders—a whole year's pay for most people in those days! Only the very rich could buy one. It was made of wood and weighed about fifty pounds. And people wore out the soles of their shoes after only a few rides. Because of rutted roads, many riders used the sidewalks, and in some cities, officials banned them from the streets.

23

Even though Karl's invention lacked the pedals of today's bicycles, it represents the first verifiable claim for a two-wheeled, steerable, human-propelled vehicle. Many people copied it, and similar machines, called velocipedes (meaning "fast foot") or boneshakers, spread through Europe and across the Atlantic.

In 1863, a French inventor added pedals. The penny-farthing or high wheeler, introduced around 1870, was the first all-metal bicycle and had solid rubber tires. The rider sat on a seat mounted directly above the high front wheel, but if a stone or rut in the road caused a sudden stop, the rider could tumble off and take a header.

There have been many iterations of the bicycle, starting with Karl's *Laufmaschine* in 1817. The word *bicycle*, meaning "two wheels," came into use in France and in the United States by the late 1860s.

Today, bicycles are one of the most important means of transportation all over the world. They led to the inventions of the the motorcycle, the car, and even the airplane. (Inventors Gottlieb Daimler, Karl Benz, and the Wright brothers loved bicycles and used bicycle technology and bicycle parts to build their innovative vehicles.) But it all started with Karl Drais, that boy who sped along the ice so long ago, dreaming of a way to travel quickly using his own two feet.

Left foot—push! Right foot—push! Steady, steady, balance!

With bicycles, women were able to travel farther by themselves. They could go to cities to compete with men for jobs, leading to more freedom and equality for women. Women's rights activists Susan B. Anthony and Elizabeth Cady Stanton declared that "woman is riding to suffrage on the bicycle." Riding a bike gave women a feeling of self-reliance. And female cyclists changed women's fashion in the late nineteenth century, introducing pants known as "bloomers" as an alternative to long dresses, which dragged on the ground and got caught in the gears.

Chapter Three

All Aboard

George Stephenson and the Steam Locomotive

link! Clunk! Hiss!

Deep underground, in a maze of pitch-black tunnels, young George Stephenson hefted chunks of coal. In the 1800s, coal not only heated homes, but it provided jobs for most of the people in the small town in England where George was growing up. *Clink* went the pickaxe. *Clunk* went the rock. *Hiss* went the steam engine that pumped water to keep the mine from flooding.

Mines were dangerous places. Miners worked in near darkness because electricity had not yet been invented, and explosions caused by torch flames injured and killed many workers. There was also a chance of flooding, as well as total collapse of the mine. Children as young as four years old sometimes worked twelve hours every day underground, pulling wagons filled with coal.

Fascinated with coal-powered steam engines, George taught himself how they worked by taking them apart and putting them back together. But he wanted to learn more.

At age nineteen, unable to read or write, he went to night school. And when he married and started a family, George was determined that his son, Robert, should get a good education. So after a full day of working in the mine, George took on more jobs, repairing shoes and fixing clocks to earn money for Robert's tuition. By candlelight, father and son ciphered sums and practiced their letters.

One day, at Killingworth colliery, a pumping engine broke. When George fixed it, the mine owner gave him a new job. Now George was the chief mechanic. It was his job to fix *all* the machinery.

Colliery: A coal mine and all its associated buildings and equipment.

But George wanted to do even more. Every day, he watched horses struggling to pull coal-filled wagons along wooden tracks. Could he find a better way to haul coal to town?

George visited a neighboring mine. He examined a steam boiler on wheels that transported coal out of the mine. Back at the colliery workshop, George tinkered with pistons and cylinders and gear wheels, and in 1814, he built a *self-moving* engine—his first steam locomotive.

Like water pumps in the coal mines, nonmoving or stationary steam engines use steam to turn gears or wheels to power machines. Locomotives or moving steam engines use steam to turn a vehicle's wheels, which pull it forward, making it travel on tracks like a train.

With George at the wheel, this locomotive hauled thirty tons of coal up a hill at four miles per hour. No horse could do that! People were excited about this new way of transporting coal. Cities were growing, and they needed food and supplies delivered faster, cheaper, and more reliably. If they could transport coal by rail, they could transport cotton and corn, too.

George wondered, What about transporting people?

For the next five years, George built locomotives—sixteen of them—each one faster than the one before. But George had a problem.

Not everyone liked his idea of transporting people by locomotive. Farmers feared that their workers would ride away to a big city to find better jobs. One day, George went to measure a field in preparation for laying the tracks. *Splash!* A crowd of farmers pushed him into a pond. *Pow! Pow! Pow!* Bullets peppered the water around him. The landowners weren't happy either. They threatened George and took him to court to keep him from laying tracks across their land. But George refused to give up. When the Stockton and Darlington Railway hired him to build twenty-five miles of track and a steam-powered locomotive, George forged ahead with his dream of transporting people by rail.

On September 27, 1825, George drove his newest engine, *Locomotion,* hauling eighty tons of coal and a newly designed passenger car. Cinders from the coal-stoked engine burned holes in ladies' shawls and men's top hats. And when the train crossed an elevated embankment at fifteen miles per hour, the passengers felt as if they were flying. But George's biggest challenge was still to come.

The Liverpool and Manchester Railway announced they were looking for the best locomotive engine to pull a very special train—for the *first regular passenger intercity rail service* from Liverpool to Manchester. The prize: five hundred pounds and a chance to build *all* the trains for the railway. George couldn't wait to get started.

First, George and his team laid the tracks. They cut tunnels, constructed bridges, and fashioned embankments. Then, he and his son designed and built *Rocket,* the fastest locomotive yet.

Before the invention of bicycles, trains, cars, and planes, most people walked wherever they had to go—at less than three miles per hour, while a horse and carriage might move along at five or six miles per hour. Many people lived their whole lives within a few miles of where they had been born.

Distribution of produce was a big problem, since roads were crowded, crooked, and bumpy. Travel by water took even longer, and goods might be lost if boats capsized during a storm.

On the day of the trials, several engines were disqualified because they were too heavy. Others broke down in the middle of the contest. But *Rocket* sped down the track, the only locomotive to complete the competition. When George and his son won the contract, they proceeded full steam ahead and in only a few months built seven more locomotives.

Allowed to run in the trials even though it was three hundred pounds over the designated weight, *Sans Pareil* cracked a cylinder and had to drop out. *Perseverance* failed to reach the required ten miles per hour and withdrew. *Cycloped* used horses walking on the drive belt for power but dropped out of the race when one of the horses fell through the floor of the engine. And the favorite, *Novelty*, suffered a broken boiler pipe that could not be fixed.

Sans Pareil

Perseverance

Cycloped

Novelty

Finally, opening day of the first intercity passenger railroad service arrived. On September 15, 1830, the band played, the crowd cheered, and the cannon sounded the signal for departure. Thousands of people watched as George's eight locomotives steamed out of Liverpool station, bound for the city of Manchester. The prime minister of England joined dozens of other dignitaries who filled the passenger cars. The railway revolution had begun, and George Stephenson had led the charge, changing the landscape not only of England but of the entire world.

Before railroads, no one had traveled faster than horses could gallop, and going farther than twenty or thirty miles was a long journey. With the advent of trains, you could travel a hundred miles to a big city in a day instead of a week. People in cities now had access to fresh milk and produce, which improved the health of city dwellers and lowered the prices of these and other commodities. The railroads unified countries and played an important part in the western expansion of the United States.

Chapter Four

Black Forest or Bust

Bertha and Karl Benz and the Gasoline-Powered Automobile

omething had to be done. And Bertha Benz was tired of waiting for her husband to do it.

Even before they were married, she had invested all her money in his company. In 1886, Karl Benz had secured a patent for a gasoline-powered horseless carriage. Bertha was sure that their Benz Patent-Motorwagens would soon be rolling down the main street of every city in Germany.

But two years had passed, and the prototype was still locked away in the workshop. Karl was afraid to take it for a long test drive.

In the 1800s, if people had to travel far, they rode by horse and carriage, by stagecoach, or by steam train, but no one had ever taken a long-distance trip in a personal motorized vehicle.

But Bertha believed in Karl. She believed in their shiny three-wheeled vehicle. Most important, Bertha believed that if people saw that the motorwagen was safe, useful, and easy to drive, they would want to buy one. So she hatched a plan.

One day in August 1888, before the cock crowed, she woke her sons, beckoned them to follow her, and tiptoed out of the house, careful not to wake her husband. She planned to drive the Patent-Motorwagen from their home in Mannheim through Germany's Black Forest to her mother's house in Pforzheim— sixty miles away.

Many feared these newfangled vehicles.

Kaiser Wilhelm II, the head of the government, feared that motorized carriages would frighten his beloved horses.

Church leaders feared that their parishioners would not come to services if they were driving around the countryside.

And pedestrians feared the vehicles and their drivers. The first time Karl drove the car around his yard, he crashed it into a brick wall.

The Benz Patent-Motorwagen was a three-wheeled automobile with a rear-mounted engine. The engine was powered by benzine, a petroleum-based product like gasoline that people used for cleaning but that also could be used as fuel. The vehicle was constructed of steel tubing with woodwork panels. The steel-spoked wheels and solid rubber tires were Karl Benz's own design.

Bertha and her sons rolled the Patent-Motorwagen out of the workshop and down the road.

She spun the flywheel.

The engine sparked.

She engaged the gear, and with many pops, shakes, and rattles, they were on their way. The roads were often bumpy and crooked. Sometimes there were no roads at all. But Bertha drove on.

Because the car did not have a cooling system, about every twelve miles, Bertha stopped to pour water over the engine so that it wouldn't overheat.

Because there were no gas stations yet and their vehicle had no gas tank, every fifteen miles or so, Bertha stopped at a pharmacy to buy bottles of benzine.

Bertha had no road maps, and she set out going the wrong way and had to take a longer route to Pforzheim. On their return trip, they went more directly. But this roundabout route turned out to be a good thing, because the more towns they drove through, the greater the number of people who saw how useful and safe the car was.

And because the car had only two gears, whenever they came to a hill, Bertha's sons hopped out and pushed while she steered, moving a crank handle because there was no steering wheel.

But Bertha drove on.

When the fuel hose clogged, Bertha whipped out her hatpin and cleared the gunk.

When the spark plug wire frayed, Bertha repaired it with her stocking garter.

And when the brake blocks wore down, Bertha stopped at a cobbler's shop and instructed the shoemaker to fashion brake pads from a piece of leather.

Going uphill was difficult; going downhill was thrilling and scary at the same time. The only way to stop the vehicle was to pull up on the large hand lever connected to wooden blocks that pressed against the back wheels, creating friction, which slowed the car down. But the friction also caused the blocks to wear away. Covering the blocks with leather protected them from wearing down and also made stopping smoother.

leather for belt/ breaks

Dusk turned to darkness. Word spread from village to village and from town to town. In those days, roads had no lights, and neither did the car. Holding lanterns to light the way, people lined the road as Bertha and her sons rattled and rolled into Pforzheim.

As soon as she could, Bertha sent a telegram to Karl, letting him know they had arrived safely.

Bertha had left a note for Karl, telling him where she was going . . . but not *how* she was getting there. She sent him several telegrams, from Bruchsal and other towns, when she stopped to get fuel and water for the car before sending him the one from Pforzheim.

But the telegram wasn't necessary. Friends had told neighbors, and neighbors had told friends, and word had reached Karl. By the time Bertha and the children returned home a few days later, the newspapers were filled with stories about the car that had traveled so many miles and the woman who had driven it.

Bertha told Karl about the problems she had encountered and how she had solved them. Karl soon outfitted his car with a fuel tank, brake pads, and a low gear for climbing hills. Other inventors, like Gottlieb Daimler and Wilhelm Maybach, were also working on gasoline-powered internal combustion engines for their horseless carriages, but Karl Benz is known as the inventor of the modern car.

Soon after Bertha returned, people started ordering the Benz Patent-Motorwagen. Bertha's road trip proved that the cars were safe and useful for everyone. More than that, she paved the way for worldwide acceptance of the automobile as a means of transportation. No longer tied to the community where they lived, people found work in other towns and cities. Over the years, new industries popped up—restaurants, and hotels and motels where tired travelers could stop for the night. And in July of 2016, exactly 125 years after a determined young woman tiptoed past her sleeping husband to take her children on a visit to their grandmother's house, Bertha Benz was inducted into the Automotive Hall of Fame in Dearborn, Michigan, in recognition of her invaluable contribution to the development and design of the modern automobile.

Chapter Five

America Gets Moving

Eric Wickman and the Interstate Bus Company

Plow. Plant. Weed.

Eric Wickman's father and grandfather were farmers. But Eric yearned to do something different. In 1905, when he turned seventeen, Eric said goodbye to Sweden and sailed to America with the equivalent of only sixty dollars in his pocket.

When he reached New York, Eric couldn't believe how many ways there were to get around the city. Elevated trains whisked passengers on tracks built high above the street. Trolleys clanged down Fifth Avenue. Horse-drawn carriages and newfangled horseless automobiles clogged roadways. Eric wanted to ride on all of them! But he needed a job, and since the territory of Arizona needed loggers, Eric boarded a train and headed west.

Farmland and forest, river and ravine, prairie and plateau flashed by. Eric loved this big, beautiful country. But getting around wasn't easy. Trains cost a lot of money. Only large cities had buses. And traveling from city to city and state to state was complicated. Eric thought someone should do something about that.

When he got to Arizona, he chopped down trees. But Eric missed hearing the voices of fellow Swedes, so he traveled to icy Minnesota to drill mines. He found Swedish friends, but before long, he lost his job.

He tried selling cars, but he couldn't sell even the one car the company had shipped to him. Times were hard. The townspeople didn't have enough money. Heads down, collars up, men and women plodded past his shop, trudging miles to work every day. Eric's mind revved with an idea.

In 1914, after buying the Hupp Motor Car Company vehicle himself, he charged twenty-five cents round-trip for a two-mile ride from the small town of Alice to the mines surrounding the city of Hibbing, sometimes cramming fifteen miners into his seven-passenger vehicle.

Train travel was expensive, but in 1905, it was the quickest way to get around a big country like America. For example, Eric's trip to Arizona cost almost forty dollars, which left him with only twenty dollars for food and other necessities until he could start working and earning money.

They filled the seats, stood on the running boards, perched on the hood, and clung to the back bumper.

Everyone loved not having to walk to work, especially in the cold weather. They traded stories, told jokes, and shared the news of the day. And no one had more fun than Eric. But soon Eric had a different kind of problem.

Too many people wanted a ride! The line stretched around the block. Eric had another idea. What if he s-t-r-e-e-t-c-h-e-d the car?

So Eric cut the car in half, added pieces of metal to make it longer, and put in extra seats.

Still it wasn't big enough.

So Eric *built* a bus. Nobody in Hibbing, Minnesota, had seen anything like it!

Eric bought a one-ton truck chassis, and together with a friend, he constructed a bus that could carry many more people than a car. As his shuttle service grew, he ordered ready-made buses.

Business boomed. Friendships bloomed.

In the winter, Eric and his passengers got out and shoveled snow together. In the spring, everyone helped push the bus out of muddy ditches. But then Eric ran into a different kind of problem.

Right down the road, someone named Ralph Bogan started a bus company just like his. That was when Eric had his biggest idea yet. He met with Ralph, and they agreed to work together, driving buses, selling tickets, repairing vehicles, and traveling to other cities to start up new bus lines.

passenger
Seats

sleeper
compartment

passenger
Seats

bathroom

In the early 1900s, there were no buses that transported passengers between cities or between states. Most people walked where they needed to go, or used a horse and carriage if they could afford it. Wagons pulled by mules were used to transport goods. Train tracks were usually laid only between major cities.

Over the next thirty years, Eric stretched his business, just like he had stretched that first car.

He joined with bus companies in other cities and states.

He partnered with train companies to provide bus service where trains couldn't go.

He added bathrooms, air-conditioning, picture windows, and the name Greyhound to his buses.

Kitchen

Driver

In June 1922, one of Eric's bus operators in Wisconsin drove past a store window. The low-slung reflection of his bus, jumping up and down, reminded him of a greyhound dog. The next week, he took his vehicle to a sign shop and had them put THE GREYHOUND just above the windows on each side. And when Eric heard about it, he knew it was the perfect name for his bus company.

Greyhound

In 1925, the president of Great Northern Railway, Ralph Budd, invested millions of dollars in Eric's company. Unlike other railroad owners who blamed buses for their dwindling sales, Ralph studied the numbers and discovered that railroad profits were just as bad in areas where there was *no* bus service. He realized it was the low-cost automobile, made possible by Henry Ford's assembly-line production of the Model T, that was to blame. He felt that railroads and buses could complement each other and not compete against each other.

Eric drove his buses until he was too old to drive. Then he rode them as a passenger. Eric loved to travel! And he wasn't the only one.

Soldiers rode Eric's buses when they moved from base to base.

Freedom Fighters rode on Eric's buses in 1961 when they protested racial discrimination in the Southern states.

And when families vacationed, Eric's buses took them north, south, east, and west.

Today, more than one hundred years later, Greyhound buses still get people where they need to go, from city to city and state to state, all across America, Mexico, and Canada.

When male drivers joined the war effort during World War II, Greyhound replaced them with female drivers, opening the door to many women who had never worked outside the home.

Chapter Six

Moon Man

Robert Goddard and the Liquid-Fuel-Propelled Rocket

ometimes Robert Goddard's curiosity was so intense, it made things explode.

When his father gave him a subscription to a magazine filled with daring experiments, Robert wanted to test them all. He read that diamonds form when carbon is exposed to extreme temperature changes. He knew graphite is a type of carbon, so he filed shavings of graphite from his pencils, heated them, and plunged them into ice-cold water. But while watching the graphite harden, he held a tube of hydrogen too close to the open flame. *Boom!*

His mother gave him a broom and a dustpan to clean up the mess.

Fascinated with flight, Robert studied kites, balloons, and birds. He filled notebooks with ideas, observations, and experiments. And he read books about electricity, physics, and chemistry, as well as science-fiction novels bursting with spaceships, heat rays, and Martian invasions.

As a boy who wanted to know how things worked, Robert wondered: *How could a spaceship escape Earth's gravity? What type of fuel would it use? And how would it move through space?*

Robert read Jules Verne's *Around the Moon* and *From the Earth to the Moon* many times. When the local newspaper published *The War of the Worlds* by H. G. Wells, Robert could hardly wait for each weekly installment.

One day, Robert climbed a cherry tree in his backyard, stared at the sky, and dreamed of traveling to Mars. By the time he climbed down, he'd made up his mind to build a device to do it!

Robert asked his teachers about space travel, but no one had answers to his questions. In those days, almost everyone believed it was impossible. So Robert studied harder. He read more. All through high school, he kept his dreams to himself but filled his journals with careful notes.

In 1903, the year before he entered college at Worcester Polytechnic Institute in Massachusetts, newspapers around the world reported the first airplane flight of the Wright brothers at Kitty Hawk, North Carolina. Robert grew even more determined to build a device that could reach the stars.

In the basement of his college physics lab, he experimented, setting off a powder-fueled rocket that filled the building with smoke.

Fortunately for Robert, no one was hurt and he was forgiven.

Robert bought Chinese rockets, fireworks, and flares. He studied their shape and design. He took them apart and put them back together. After college, he built his own rockets—but none of them flew.

Finding just the right fuel wasn't Robert's only problem. Rocket supplies cost money. Hoping for support from the Smithsonian Institution in Washington, DC, Robert wrote a report called "A Method of Reaching Extreme Altitudes." He explained how his rockets could be used to send weather-recording instruments into the atmosphere *much higher* than a research balloon. He also mentioned the possibility of the rocket reaching the moon.

Newspapers made fun of him. They called him the Moon Man.

But the Smithsonian gave him a grant of five thousand dollars. Now Robert had money to build and test more rockets. In a warehouse, behind closed doors and with blankets covering the windows for privacy, Robert developed a system for pumping liquid oxygen and gasoline into the engine of his rocket so that the fuel would cool the engine and keep it from melting. He proved that rockets *could* work beyond Earth's atmosphere, calculating the speed a rocket must travel in order to escape Earth's gravitational pull. And he even came up with the idea of using gyroscopes for rocket stability.

A gyroscope is a spinning wheel on an axle. Once the device is spinning, it resists changes to its orientation. It was invented in 1852 by Léon Foucault to help him study the rotation of the earth.

From Robert's journals: "All rockets are cylindrical. All rockets are tapered at the top and flat at the bottom where the exhaust gases are forced out. All rockets are smooth and straight along the sides. The narrower the nozzle at the bottom, the more pressure [is] created inside the rocket and the greater the thrust that [powers] it upward."

Then, on March 16, 1926, in the meadow behind his aunt's farm-house in Auburn, Massachusetts, Robert attempted to fly his rocket again. He wrote in his diary:

Tried rocket at 2:30. It rose 41 ft, & went 184 ft, in 2.5 secs.

He had successfully launched the first liquid-fuel-propelled rocket!

During the next four years, Robert Goddard built rocket after rocket.

Gas tanks exploded. Valves melted. Combustion chambers burned. But Robert refused to give up.

On July 17, 1929, Robert loaded a rocket with a camera, a barometer, and a thermometer. It soared one hundred feet into the air, until . . .

Boom!

The gas tank blew up with a noise that was heard for miles. Neighbors, firefighters, and reporters hurried to the scene. And again, the press mocked Robert with a newspaper headline that read: "Moon Rocket Misses Target by 238,799½ Miles."

But the explosion also drew the attention of another lover of aeronautics, Charles Lindbergh, who only two years earlier had completed the first solo airplane flight from New York to Paris.

Charles came to visit Robert. He believed in Robert's dream of space travel. And it wasn't long before Charles arranged for supplies and a better place for Robert to continue improving his rockets.

Robert understood that it was hard for most people to accept his ideas. He said, "Every vision is a joke until the first man accomplishes it; once realized, it becomes commonplace."

Robert Goddard

Over the next fifteen years, Robert blazed a trail in rocket science. He is credited with 214 patents, including his 1914 patents for the multistage rocket and his liquid-fueled rocket, both milestones in the development of rocketry, inspiring others to believe that space travel was possible.

And although he died in 1945, long before satellites circled the earth and astronauts walked on the moon, Robert Goddard ushered in the era of space flight with the world's first liquid-fuel-propelled rocket. Today's space program is built on the discoveries he made, and for some of us, that trip to Mars young Robert dreamed about up in the cherry tree may one day become a reality.

Chapter Seven

Herbert and Harry Find a Way

Herbert Everest and Harry Jennings
and the Folding Wheelchair

othing stopped Herbert Everest when he set his mind to something. Sunshine or rain, he took daring road trips in his old jalopy. At school, he raced around the track and jumped high hurdles. And after he graduated from college in 1908, he worked as a mining engineer, tunneling through dirt and rock underground.

But one April day in 1918, while he was working as a mine superintendent for the Southern Anthracite Coal Company, a fire broke out. The mine filled with burning timbers, blistering heat, and rumbling, bone-crushing boulders.

When the dust cleared and they carried Herbert out of the mine, his back was broken.

Paralyzed, Herbert Everest faced the knowledge that the days of road trips in his old jalopy were over. His legs would never race around the track or clear the high hurdles. He could not even walk.

For two years, Herbert lay in bed, too badly injured to read or write. For two years, his wife and daughter cared for him. Finally, his outer bruises healed. But his severed spine could not be fixed. Confined to a wheelchair, he sat.

One day, Herbert's friend Harry Jennings came to visit. Harry paid attention as Herbert complained about the bulky wheelchair that kept him prisoner.

It was certainly better than the Bath chair, invented in 1783, which weighed so much it had to be pulled by a donkey or a horse. But Herbert's wheelchair was still too heavy for his wife to carry outside so he could sit in the garden. And while his chair could move, it was too big to go through doorways and would *never* fit into an automobile.

The first known wheelchair specifically designed for disability was invented in 1595 for King Philip II of Spain. The chair had small wheels, a platform for the king's feet, and an adjustable backrest. It was heavy and cumbersome and required a strong, healthy person to push it.

Harry Jennings wanted to help. He was not only Herbert's friend, he was also a mechanical engineer who loved to make and fix things. He spent days tinkering in his garage.

Herbert had said his wheelchair was too heavy. So Harry built a frame from steel aircraft tubing instead of wood.

Herbert had told him his wheelchair was too big, so Harry sawed and snipped!

Most important, Herbert wanted a wheelchair that could fit in a car. But Harry couldn't figure out how to manage that.

Back to Herbert's house he went. The two friends brainstormed. Their minds bubbled with ideas. To fit into a car, the chair would have to fold up, like an umbrella or a seat in a theater.

Then Herbert remembered the camp chair he had used in the mines, with an X-brace design, a hinged seat, and a collapsing metal frame.

Together, Herbert Everest and Harry Jennings bent and flared the tubing, twisted and welded the joints, and cut and stitched the fabric for the seat.

In 1932, they created a revolutionary type of wheelchair: made of metal and weighing only fifty pounds instead of one hundred, it folded neatly for easy transportation.

What do actor Christopher Reeve, President Franklin Delano Roosevelt, and English Prime Minister Winston Churchill have in common? They all used wheelchairs manufactured by Everest & Jennings.

No longer a prisoner in his home, Herbert took his beloved road trips again, visited hospitals to talk to injured war veterans, and hired disabled people to work in his wheelchair company.

The Ever-Rest folding wheelchair, the prototype for modern wheelchairs, allowed disabled individuals to use their chair outside their homes or care facilities. Among many other honors, Herbert's company received a Presidential Citation in 1948 for hiring the differently abled, and he was awarded the Distinguished Achievement Medal from the Colorado School of Mines for his utilization of his engineering training for the benefit of those unable to walk. And in 1956, Everest & Jennings became the first company to successfully market the power chair.

Over the years, Herbert and Harry and other inventors improved the design of wheelchairs, making them more comfortable and more functional. Today there are electric wheelchairs, chairs that climb stairs, and chairs that lift and support the user in a standing position. And at the Paralympics, athletes from around the world compete in chairs designed specifically for each sport.

electric wheelchair

Stair-climbing wheelchair

Standing wheelchair

Paraplegic wheelchair

The Paralympics have grown to include more than four thousand athletes participating in almost two dozen sports, including wheelchair tennis, basketball, and fencing.

Chapter Eight

The Birth of Robotics

George Devol and the Industrial Robot

From the time he was a boy, George Devol's favorite place was a garage full of springs, sprockets, and gears.

At age fifteen, he rebuilt the transmission on the family car—without any instructions. While other kids played sports, George read everything he could find on engineering and science fiction. Especially science fiction. Novels like *The War of the Worlds* by H. G. Wells. Comics like Buck Rogers. Images of robots and fantastic machines leaped off the pages. George daydreamed about making science fiction come alive.

Not content to merely dream, George continued to tinker after he finished high school. Every day, his ideas percolated. One by one, new inventions were born. He produced the first doors to automatically open and close. And he created the first photoelectronic entrance counter (for counting the number of people entering a building or area), which he demonstrated at New York's World's Fair in 1939.

One day, George was flipping through a factory manual. A photo of workers on an assembly line captured his attention. Each worker was receiving objects or parts on a conveyer belt. Each person did one job, and then the object or part continued down the conveyer belt to the next worker on the line. Each worker did the same job over and over throughout the day.

George thought if a machine could do those repetitive jobs, workers' lives could be improved. He pictured a machine like a human arm with a wrist that rotated and a hand that could grab things, lift them, and move them from place to place. He built the prototype and tested it. The machine grabbed a can of paint and held on tight.

Tighter.

Too tight!

Squish!

Paint splattered everywhere. George would have to do something about that.

He installed pressure sensors inside the machine's hand. Now the machine would know how hard to grip based on the weight of the item it picked up. But building the machine wasn't George's biggest challenge. He had to find someone to *buy* it. And George was an inventor, not a salesman. For years, he approached one company president after another and heard *No* in many different languages, from *Nyet* (in Russian) to *Bu* (in Chinese) to *Nahi* (in Hindi).

Then something happened that changed everything.

At a party, George met Joseph Engelberger, a young engineer and entrepreneur. They talked for hours about their favorite author, Isaac Asimov, and his fictional robots.

Isaac Asimov introduced the Three Laws of Robotics in his 1942 short story "Runaround."

1. A robot may not injure a human being or, through inaction, allow a human being to come to harm.

2. A robot must obey orders given it by human beings, except where such orders would conflict with the First Law.

3. A robot must protect its own existence as long as such protection does not conflict with the First or Second Law.

He later added another law, the zeroth, which comes before the other three:

0. A robot may not harm humanity, or, by inaction, allow humanity to come to harm.

When Joseph asked what kind of work George did, George told him about his latest invention, the mechanical arm that gripped cans, drilled holes, and sprayed paint. Joseph's eyes lit with excitement. Human workers would be safer and happier if dull, difficult, and dangerous jobs could be done by machines. And a machine could work all day and all night and never ask for a bathroom break. "Sounds like a robot to me," he told his new friend.

George and Joseph soon joined in a business venture they called Unimation. It was the first robotics company in the world! George would handle production of the robot. Joseph would sell it.

Joseph faced serious challenges. Workers feared they would lose their jobs if robots could do everything. And some people just feared robots. In many movies and books, humanlike robots wanted to destroy the world. To help people become more comfortable with the idea of automated labor, Joseph appeared on television shows with the Unimation robot, which putted golf balls into a cup.

Finally, in 1961, at a New Jersey General Motors automobile factory, the first Unimation robot went into action. It gripped red-hot handles, dropped them into pools of cooling liquid, and welded them to doors as an assembly line moved cars along to workers who no longer had to touch sizzling metal parts.

Today, millions of industrial robots work around the clock in factories all over the world. Robotic devices record our TV shows, clean our homes, play our music, and even run our cars. And the mechanical arm that squashed a can of paint has become a prototype for the robotic devices used as prostheses for people who have lost arms or legs. In 2011, George Devol was inducted into the US National Inventors Hall of Fame. The citation reads, "George Devol's patent for the first digitally operated programmable robotic arm represents the foundation of the modern robotics industry." The boy who daydreamed about turning science fiction into reality had succeeded, helping not only factory workers on assembly lines, but also women, men, and children all over the world.

Not only did the robot keep human workers safer, it sped up production. And the faster cars were built, the cheaper they became.

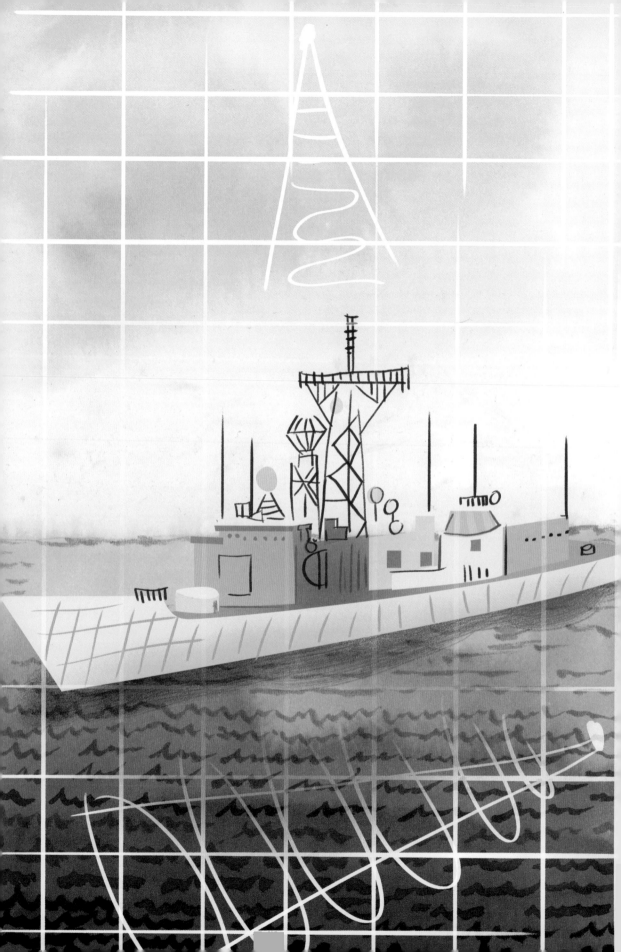

Chapter Nine

Raye Draws Her Own Lines

Raye Montague and Computer-Generated Ship Design

When Raye Montague was seven years old, she knew exactly what she wanted to be when she grew up.

In 1942, while taking a tour of a captured enemy submarine, she peered through the periscope. She admired the gleaming dials on the control panel. Raye wondered what kind of job she'd need in order to operate a submarine. So she asked the tour guide.

"Oh, you'd have to be an engineer," he told her. "But you don't ever have to worry about that."

At that time, most people expected girls to get married and have a family when they grew up. But right then and there, Raye made up her mind to become an engineer. When she got home, Raye asked her mother to help her find out what she would have to study to become an engineer. They learned that Raye would have to take lots of math and science. She was ready.

In grade school, with segregation the law of the land in most Southern towns, Raye read from hand-me-down books and sat at well-worn desks. But one of her teachers told her, "Aim for the stars, and, at the very worst, you will land on the moon." Raye took those words to heart.

When Raye was a girl, her mother told her, "Raye, you'll have three strikes against you. You're female and you're black, and you have a Southern, segregated-school education. But you can be or do anything you want . . . provided you're educated." Raye never forgot those words.

In high school, Raye knew she would have to work ten times harder if she wanted a job that was usually reserved for white men. She joined the debate team and the mathematics club and was inducted into the National Honor Society.

In college, Raye listened to Professor Simon Haley tell stories about his son, Alex, who was breaking the color barrier in the field of journalism. Raye thought if he could break barriers, so could she. But when she graduated from college in 1956 with a degree in business—because the only school in Arkansas that offered a degree in engineering did not accept minorities—opportunities for young black women were limited to jobs like teaching in a school for black children, cleaning homes for white folks, or laboring on a farm or in a factory. Many people thought Raye should give up on her dream.

At Raye's high school, girls took four years of home economics, where they learned to take care of a home and family, while boys took four years of shop, where they designed and built things. Raye wanted to take shop. Her mother went to Raye's school and was told that if Raye could pass the home economics test, she could take shop instead. Raye aced the test.

But the day after graduation, she packed her bags and boarded a train for Washington, DC. Soon she began working for the US Navy as a clerk.

Day after day, Raye sat and typed. Day after day, she watched Ivy League–graduate engineers run the UNIVAC, the first commercial computer produced in the United States. And day after day, when she left work, she attended classes in computer programming. Raye was determined to learn everything an engineer needed to know.

One day, all the engineers called in sick. Raye ran the UNIVAC by herself. Her supervisors couldn't believe it.

For years afterward, Raye did all the same tasks her male coworkers did. But she was told she would have to work the night shift if she wanted a promotion. Raye was willing, even though buses didn't run late enough. She saved $375 and bought a used car so that she could travel to work at any time of the day or night. She got a job working the night shift, but Raye still had one big problem.

She didn't know how to drive a car. She knew only how to start and stop it.

"I'd leave home about ten o'clock and I'd drive no-mile-an-hour," she said. "And then, the next morning . . . I'd hang around until about nine thirty for the traffic to let up."

Raye got her promotion and soon took charge of a team of engineers. Still, she struggled every day to prove herself. Then something extraordinary happened.

In 1970, during the Vietnam War, President Richard Nixon wanted the US Navy to design a new type of boat—a frigate that could carry missiles. It was a high priority, so he wanted it done *fast!* He ordered the navy to design the ship in two months—it usually took about two years.

The admirals heard that Raye and her team were creating a computer program that could design a ship. They challenged her to finish the job in one month.

Designing a ship was a time-consuming process. But the program Raye and her team created drastically reduced the time needed.

Minute by minute, Raye and her team checked specifications. Hour after hour, they input data. And after eighteen hours and fifty-six minutes, they produced a rough draft for the USS *Oliver Hazard Perry,* a guided-missile frigate—and the first ship designed by computer!

Raye never earned an engineering degree, but she picked up skills on the job and while attending night school. She was able to become a registered professional engineer in both the United States and Canada by acing the tests.

From that point on, Raye and her team revolutionized the way ships were designed. And she received the Society of Manufacturing Engineers Achievement Award, becoming the first female professional engineer to do so.

The tour director had been right all those long years ago. Raye didn't need to *worry* about becoming an engineer . . .

. . . she just went out and *did* it!

Raye was the US Navy's first female program manager of ships. She held the civilian equivalent of the rank of captain. Legislation like the 1964 Civil Rights Act and the 1965 Voting Rights Act made racial segregation and discrimination illegal, but it took courageous individuals like Raye Montague to put those new laws to the test and break through the barriers that had been impenetrable for so many years.

 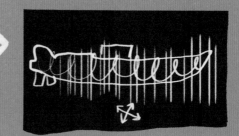

Raye Montague didn't rest on her laurels. She was always on the lookout for people who deserved promotions. She found college graduates with degrees in mathematics working in mailrooms and recommended them for positions better suited to their qualifications. "Open doors for other people," Raye said. "Become a master of the game . . . and get inside the system so you can help change the rules. You have to change the rules so you can open the doors."

Build Your Dream

When Joseph-Armand Bombardier was fifteen, he mounted the engine of a Ford Model T onto four wooden runners, perched a handmade propeller on the back, and created the first snowmobile, which he patented in 1936. But Joseph wanted more—or less. And for the next fourteen years, he slimmed it down until, in 1954, he patented the Ski-Doo, an ultra-light snowmobile used for recreation and rescue. Kylie Simonds was only eight when she designed the I-Pack, a portable IV machine that can be placed in a backpack to give kids more freedom to move around if they need chemotherapy or other IV treatment like she did. And in 2015, a team of teenagers created the SMARTwheel device to encourage better driving habits and improve automobile safety. It snaps onto any car steering wheel and uses lights and sounds to tell drivers when they are distracted and not paying attention to the road.

Have you dreamed up a new idea?

To find out more about how to take your dream to the next level and to connect with kid-friendly organizations that encourage inventive minds, check out the following resources:

- Design Squad: pbskids.org/designsquad
  Resources for kids to find engineering, science, and technology activities, plus links for parents and teachers.

- Google Science Fair: www.googlesciencefair.com
  Worldwide online competition, open to individuals or teams, ages 13 to 18.

- Kid Inventors' Day: www.kidinventorsday.com
  Website that encourages kids to be inventors. Find links for kids, teachers, and parents.

- Reading Rockets: www.readingrockets.org/article/think-inventor
  Activity page with ideas to spark creative thinking and also a list of recommended books about inventors.

- Young Inventors' Program: www.aas-world.org/YIP
  Inspires students to look at their world differently through participation in either the Invention Convention or the Rube Goldberg Contest.

- Young Inventor Challenge: www.chitag.com/yic
  Offers an opportunity for children ages 6 to 18 to showcase their own original toy and game inventions.

Source Notes

Introduction

9 "Life is like riding": Walter Isaacson, *Einstein: His Life and His Universe* (New York: Simon & Schuster, 2007), 367.

Chapter One: Boys Who Dream of Flying

17 "We observed it lift off ": "The Fabulous Story of the First Hot-Air Balloon Flights," August 5, 2016 (www.faena.com/aleph/articles/the-fabulous-story-of-the-first-hot-air-balloon-flights).

Chapter Two: With His Own Two Feet

25 "Woman is riding to suffrage": "Champion of Her Sex: Miss Susan B. Anthony Tells the Story of Her Remarkable Life to 'Nellie Bly,' " *World,* New York, February 2, 1896, 10.

Chapter Six: Moon Man

55 "All rockets are cylindrical": Streissguth, *Rocket Man*, 23.

56 "Tried rocket at 2:30": Robert Goddard's diary, March 16, 1926 (www2.clarku.edu/research/archives/goddard/diary.cfm).

"Moon Rocket Misses Target": Oliver Moody, "Review: The Earth Gazers by Christopher Potter," *Times,* August 26, 2017 (www.thetimes.co.uk/article/review-the-earth-gazers-by-christopher-potter-5tplrtbfh).

"Every vision is a joke": NASA, "Robert Goddard: A Man and His Rocket," March 9, 2004 (www.nasa.gov/missions/research/f_goddard.html).

Chapter Eight: The Birth of Robotics

69 A robot may not injure: Isaac Asimov, "The Runaround," in *I, Robot* (New York: Bantam Books, 2008), 37.

70 "Sounds like a robot": Robotic Industries Association, "Unimate—The First Industrial Robot."

71 "George Devol's patent for the first": Davidson, "Father of Robotics."

Chapter Nine: Raye Draws Her Own Lines

73 "Oh, you'd have to be": Miller, "Meet the Woman Who Broke Barriers."

74 "Aim for the stars": Raye Montague, interview by Jajuan Johnson, Butler Center for Arkansas Studies, January 29, 2009 (cdm15728.contentdm.oclc.org/cdm/ref/collection/p1532coll1/id/12700).

"Raye, you'll have three strikes": Miller, "Meet the Woman Who Broke Barriers."

76 "I'd leave home about": Collins, "Breaking Barriers, Part 2."

79 "Open doors for": Collins, "Breaking Barriers, Part 2."

Selected Bibliography

Smithsonian National Air and Space Museum (NASM 9A08390)

Chapter One: Boys Who Dream of Flying

Bristow, David. *Sky Sailors: True Stories of the Balloon Era.* New York: Farrar, Straus and Giroux, 2010.

Crouch, Tom. "Runaway Balloons." Smithsonian National Air and Space Museum. October 21, 2009. (airandspace.si.edu/stories/editorial/runaway-balloons)

Evans, Charles M. *The War of the Aeronauts: A History of Ballooning during the Civil War.* Mechanicsburg, PA: Stackpole Books, 2002.

Gillispie, Charles Coulston. *The Montgolfier Brothers and the Invention of Aviation: 1783–1784.* Princeton, NJ: Princeton University Press, 1983.

Hagedorn, Dan, and Sheila Keenan. *The Story of Flight: Early Flying Machines, Balloons, Blimps, Gliders, Warplanes, and Jets.* New York: Scholastic, 1995.

Latson, Jennifer. "A Sheep, a Duck and a Rooster in a Hot-Air Balloon—No Joke." *Time,* November 21, 2014. (time.com/3583782/hot-air-balloon-history)

Lausanne, Edita. *The Romance of Ballooning: The Story of the Early Aeronauts.* New York: Viking, 1971.

The Museum of Flight. "The Montgolfier Brothers' Balloon." (museumofflight.org/exhibits/montgolfier-brothers-balloon; accessed January 9, 2016)

Priceman, Marjorie. *Hot Air: The (Mostly) True Story of the First Hot-Air Balloon Ride.* New York: Atheneum for Young Readers, 2005.

The Robinson Library. "The Montgolfier Brothers." (robinsonlibrary.com/technology/motor/aeronautics/balloons/montgolfier.htm; accessed January 9, 2016)

Smithsonian Libraries. "Age of the Aeronaut." (library.si.edu/exhibition/fantastic-worlds/age-of-the-aeronaut; accessed March 27, 2018)

Today in Science History. "The Montgolfier Brothers, Pioneer Balloonists." (todayinsci.com/M/Montgolfier_Brothers/Montgolfier_Brothers.htm; accessed January 9, 2016)

University of Bristol School of Chemistry. "Lighter Than Air: The Montgolfier Brothers." (www.chm.bris.ac.uk/webprojects2003/hetherington/final/montgolfier_bros.html; accessed January 9, 2016)

Chapter Two: With His Own Two Feet

Painting of Karl von Drais on his original *Laufmaschine*, or draisine, the earliest two-wheeler, in 1819, artist unknown

Alfred, Randy. "Proto-Bicycle Gets Things Rolling." *Wired,* February 17, 2011. (www.wired.com/2011/02/0217draisine-sauerbrun-bicycle-forerunner)

Brown University Joukowsky Institute for Archaeology and the Ancient World. "History of the Bicycle: A Timeline." (brown.edu/Departments/Joukowsky_Institute/courses/13things/7083.html; accessed December 17, 2017)

Guroff, Margaret. *The Mechanical Horse: How the Bicycle Reshaped American Life.* Austin: University of Texas, 2016.

Haduch, Bill, and Chris Murphy. *Go Fly a Bike! The Ultimate Book About Bicycle Fun, Freedom & Science.* New York: Dutton Children's Books, 2004.

Hamer, Mike. "Brimstone and Bicycles." *New Scientist,* January 26, 2005. (www.newscientist.com/article/mg18524841-900-brimstone-and-bicycles)

Herlihy, David V. *Bicycle: The History.* New Haven, CT: Yale University Press, 2006.

Hoefer, Carsten. "A Short Illustrated History of the Bicycle." *Crazy Guy on a Bike.* (www.crazyguyonabike.com/doc/page/?page_id=40616; accessed July 7, 2017)

Klingaman, William K., and Nicolas P. Klingaman. *The Year Without Summer: 1816 and the Volcano That Darkened the World and Changed History.* New York: St. Martin's Press, 2013.

Mozer, David. "Bicycle History (& Human Powered Vehicle History)." International

Bicycle Fund. (www.ibike.org/library/history-timeline.htm; accessed July 1, 2017)

Chapter Three: All Aboard

George Stephenson's *Rocket*, the locomotive built by Robert Stephenson, University of California Libraries

American-Rails. "Stephenson's *Rocket*." (www.american-rails.com/stephensons-rocket.html; accessed August 20, 2017)

Chant, Christopher. *Marshall Cavendish Illustrated Guide to Steam Locomotives*. Marshall Cavendish Corp, 1991.

Ducksters Education Site. "Industrial Revolution: Steam Engine." (www.ducksters.com/history/us_1800s/steam_engine_industrial_revolution.php; accessed August 10, 2017)

Engineering Timelines. "George Stephenson." (engineering-timelines.com/who/Stephenson_G/stephensonGeorge.asp; accessed August 3, 2017)

Kalla-Bishop, P. M., and Luciano Greggio. *Steam Locomotives*. Wingdale, NY: Crescent Books, 1985.

"The Rocket—Replica of Stephenson's 1829 Steam Locomotive." YouTube. April 19, 2010. (www.youtube.com/watch?v=yNn0LC_9imY)

Trueman, C. N. "Coal Mines in the Industrial Revolution." The History Learning Site. March 31, 2015. (www.historylearningsite.co.uk/britain-1700-to-1900/industrial-revolution/coal-mines-in-the-industrial-revolution)

Wolmar, Christian. *The Iron Road: An Illustrated History of the Railroad*. New York: DK, 2014.

Zimmermann, Karl. *Steam Locomotives: Whistling, Chugging, Smoking Iron Horses of the Past*. Honesdale, PA: Boyds Mills Press, 2004.

Chapter Four: Black Forest or Bust

Conradt, Stacy. "Bertha Benz and the First-Ever Road Trip." *Mental Floss*, May 1, 2015. (mentalfloss.com/article/63226/bertha-benz-and-first-ever-road-trip)

First gas-powered automobile, Mercedes-Benz Classic Archives

Crain, Keith. "Honoring 4 worthy hall of famers." *Automotive News*, July 18, 2016.

Daimler Motors. "August 1888: Bertha Benz Takes World's First Long-Distance Trip in an Automobile." (media.daimler.com/marsMediaSite/en/instance/ko/August-1888-Bertha-Benz-takes-worlds-first-long-distance-trip-in-an-automobile.xhtml?oid=9361401; accessed February 10, 2018)

Frankel, Andrew. "Happy Birthday Bertha Benz—the Woman at the Wheel of the First Ever Road Trip." *The Telegraph*, May 3, 2017. (www.telegraph.co.uk/motoring/10275540/Bertha-Benz-the-mother-of-motoring.html)

Maranzani, Barbara. "Bertha Benz Hits the Road." A&E Television Networks, August 5, 2013. (www.history.com/news/bertha-benz-hits-the-road)

Tweney, Dylan. "Aug. 12, 1888: Road Trip! Berta Takes the Benz." *Wired,* December 8, 2010. (www.wired.com/2010/08/0812berta-benz-first-road-trip)

Wüst, Christian. "Germany's New Mercedes Museum: From Horsepower to the Popemobile." *Spiegel,* May 18, 2006. (www.spiegel.de/international/spiegel/germany-s-new-mercedes-museum-from-horsepower-to-the-popemobile-a-416896.html)

Chapter Five: America Gets Moving

Alsing, Peter. "Martis Jerk—Buskungen from Våmhus." Translated by Google Translate. Last modified August 8, 2015. (alsing.com/greyhound)

Ascher, Charlie. "From a Single Hupmobile to a Fleet of 1,552 Buses, Greyhound Turns 100." *Hemmings Daily,* August 14, 2014. (blog.hemmings.com/index.php/2014/08/14/from-a-single-hupmobile-to-a-fleet-of-1552-buses-greyhound-turns-100)

Belsky, Gary. "100 Years on a Dirty Dog: The History of Greyhound." *Mental Floss,* December 19, 2013. (mentalfloss.com/article/54273/100-years-dirty-dog-history-greyhound)

"Carl Wickman, Greyhound Bus Founder, Dead." *Chicago Tribune,* February 6, 1954. (archives.chicagotribune.com/1954/02/06/page/23/article/carl-wickman-greyhound-bus-founder-dead)

Deal Books. Lehman Brothers Collection. Baker Library. "The Greyhound Corporation." (www.library.hbs.edu/hc/lehman/company. html?company=the_greyhound_corporation; accessed February 25, 2018)

Forgione, Mary. "Celebrating 100 Years, Greyhound Turns Two Buses into Mobile Museum." *Los Angeles Times,* April 14, 2014. (www.latimes.com/ travel/la-trb-greyound-100-anniversary-tour-20140609-story.html)

Jackson, Carlton. *Hounds of the Road: A History of the Greyhound Bus Company.* 2nd ed. Bowling Green, OH: Bowling Green State University Popular Press, 2001.

Lynch, Jack. "Boys Watched the Hup Come to Town." *Hibbing Daily Tribune*, July 5, 2015.

Eric Wickman's first Hupmobile, Greyhound Lines, INC

Palermo, Diane. Interview by author. Telephone and email. February 2016 and March 2016 (emails) and December 2016 (phone conversation).

Pirelli Tyres. "Greyhound Bus: The Way to Live the America on the Road." November 26, 2015. (www.pirelli.com/global/ en-ww/life/america-on-the-road)

Plachno, Larry. "Greyhound Buses Through the Years." Parts I and II. *National Bus Trader,* September 2002. (www.daverothacker.com/files/greyh1-1.pdf and www.daverothacker.com/files/greyh2.pdf)

Roberts, Kate. "The Greyhound Bus Company." *Minnesota 150: The People, Places, and Things That Shape Our State.* St. Paul: Minnesota Historical Society Press, 2007.

Walsh, Margaret. "Tracing the Hound: The Minnesota Roots of the Greyhound Bus Company." *Minnesota History*, Winter 1985. (collections.mnhs.org/ MNHistoryMagazine/articles/49/v49i08p310-321.pdf)

Washington, Robin. "Can 'Mr. Greyhound' Add a Little History to Museum?" *Duluth News Times,* June 7, 2009. (www.duluthnewstribune.com/business/ transportation/2284745-can-mr-greyhound-add-little-history-museum)

"Wickman Opened a Hupmobile Dealership." *Bus Digest Magazine*, August 1, 2013. (busdigest.blogspot.com/2013/08/in-1914-laid-off-miner-named-carl.html)

Chapter Six: Moon Man

Bankston, John. *Robert Goddard and the Liquid Rocket Engine*. Hallandale, FL: Mitchell Lane Publishers, 2002.

Brown, David E., et al. *Inventing Modern America: From the Microwave to the Mouse*. Reprint ed. Cambridge, MA: The MIT Press, 2003.

Clary, David A. *Rocket Man: Robert H. Goddard and the Birth of the Space Age*. New York: Hyperion, 2003.

Goddard, Robert. "Autobiographical Statement 1921." Robert Hutchings Goddard Library. Clark University. (database.goddard.microsearch.net/Contents; accessed March 24, 2018)

———. "Notebook of Robert Goddard 1908–1912." Robert Hutchings Goddard Library. Clark University. (database.goddard.microsearch.net/Contents; accessed March 24, 2018)

American rocketry pioneer Robert H. Goddard and his first liquid-fueled rocket, March 16, 1926, courtesy NASA/JPL-Caltech

NASA. "Dr. Robert H. Goddard, American Rocketry Pioneer." Last modified August 3, 2017. (www.nasa.gov/centers/goddard/about/history/dr_goddard.html)

Neufeld, Michael J., and Alex M. Spencer, eds. *Smithsonian National Air and Space Museum: An Autobiography*. Washington, D.C.: National Geographic, 2010.

Redd, Nola Taylor. "Robert Goddard: American Father of Rocketry." Space.com. February 25, 2013. (www.space.com/19944-robert-goddard.html)

Roberts, Russell. *Robert Goddard: Rocket Man*. Hallandale, FL: Mitchell Lane Publishers, 2005.

Spilsbury, Louise A. *Robert Goddard and the Rocket*. New York: PowerKids Press, 2016.

Streissguth, Thomas. *Rocket Man: The Story of Robert Goddard*. Minneapolis: Carolrhoda Books, 1995.

Chapter Seven: Herbert and Harry Find a Way

Anderson, Rachel. "History of the Wheelchair." *Where It's At* (blog). Ability Tools, October 11, 2013. (abilitytools.org/blog/history-of-the-wheelchair)

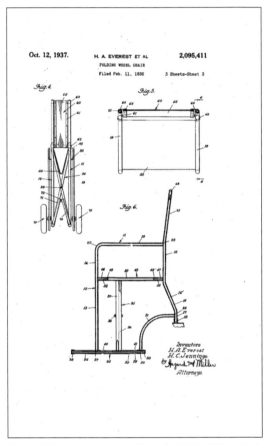

Everest, Herbert A., Jennings, Harry C., Folding Wheelchair, US2095411A, United States Patent and Trademark Office

Bakhshi, Joe. "Wheelchair Facts, Numbers and Figures [Infographic]." Smart Chair. January 29, 2015. (kdsmartchair.com/blogs/news/18706123-wheelchair-facts-numbers-and-figures-infographic)

British Healthcare Trades Association. "Everest and Jennings Wheelchairs Corby (1977)." February 27, 2017. (bhta.com/everest-and-jennings-wheelchairs-corby-1977)

Everest, Herbert C., and Harry C. Jennings. "US2095411A—Folding Wheel Chair." Google Patents. Accessed March 6, 2018. (patents.google.com/patent/US2095411)

Florence, Erin. "Wheeling Thru Time: The History of the Wheelchair." *A Cup of Cocoa and a Chinwag*, July 29, 2012. (cocoaandchinwag.wordpress.com/2012/07/29/wheeling-thru-time-the-history-of-the-wheelchair/#more-1597)

Fritsch, Kelly. "Beyond the Wheelchair: Rethinking the Politics of Disability and Accessibility." *Briarpatch*. March 10, 2014. (briarpatchmagazine.com/articles/view/beyond-the-wheelchair)

"In Memoriam for Herbert Austin Everest." *Mines Magazine* 50 (January 1960): 37.

International Paralympic Committee. "The IPC—Who We Are: Paralympics History—History of the Paralympic Movement." (paralympic.org/the-ipc/history-of-the-movement; accessed March 7, 2018)

Kelly, Kate. "The Wheelchair: Who Thought of It?" *America Comes Alive*. May 19, 2016. (americacomesalive.com/2016/05/19/the-wheelchair-who-thought-of-it)

Kleinfield, N. R. "Wheelchair Maker vs. Critics." *New York Times*, February 12, 1981.

Chapter Eight: The Birth of Robotics

Baker, Christopher W. *Robots Among Us: The Challenges and Promises of Robotics*. Minneapolis: Millbrook Press, 2002.

Ballard, Leslie Anne, et al. "George Charles Devol, Jr. [History]." IEEE Xplore Digital Library. September 11, 2012. (ieeexplore.ieee.org/document/6299167)

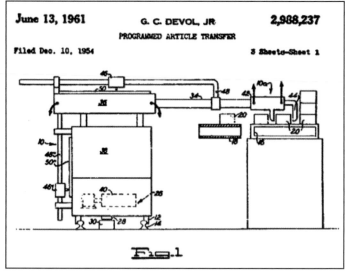

Devol, Jr., George C., Programmed Article Transfer, US2988237A, United States Patent and Trademark Office

Chaline, Eric. *Fifty Machines That Changed the Course of History*. Allston, MA: Firefly Books, 2012.

Davidson, Phil. "Father of Robotics Who Helped to Revolutionise Carmaking." *Financial Times*. August 19, 2011.

Devol, George. *Programmed Article Transfer*. 1961. US Patent #2,988,237. (patents.google.com/patent/US2988237A/en)

Hyland, Tony. *Robots at Work and Play*. North Mancato, MN: Smart Apple Media, 2008.

Ichbiah, Daniel. *Robots: From Science Fiction to Technological Revolution*. New York: Harry N. Abrams, 2005.

MacEachern, Frank. "Robotics Pioneer George Devol, a Former Greenwich Resident, Dies at 99." *CT Post,* August 16, 2011. (ctpost.com/local/article/Robotics-pioneer-George-Devol-a-former-Greenwich-2076055.php)

Malone, Bob. "George Devol: A Life Devoted to Invention, and Robots." IEEE Spectrum. September 26, 2011. (spectrum.ieee.org/automaton/robotics/industrial-robots/george-devol-a-life-devoted-to-invention-and-robots)

McGrath, Dylan. "Farewell, Joe Engelberger." *EETimes,* December 5, 2015. (www.eetimes.com/author.asp?section_id=36&doc_id=1328428)

Mitchell, Oliver. "Robots Mourn Their Creator." *Chronicling the Robot Industry.* August 16, 2011. (robotrabbi.com/tag/speedy-weeny)

Moran, Michael E. "Evolution of Robotic Arms." *Journal of Robotic Surgery* 2007 1(2): 103–111. (www.ncbi.nlm.nih.gov/pmc/articles/PMC4247431)

Pearce, Jeremy. "George Devol, Inventor of Robot Arm, Dies at 99." *New York Times,* August 16, 2011. (www.nytimes.com/2011/08/16/business/george-devol-developer-of-robot-arm-dies-at-99.html)

Robotic Industries Association."Unimate—The First Industrial Robot." *A Tribute to Joseph Engelberger.* (www.robotics.org/joseph-engelberger/unimate.cfm; accessed April 4, 2018)

Rosen, Rebecca J. "Unimate: The Story of George Devol and the First Robotic Arm." *The Atlantic*, August 16, 2011. (www.theatlantic.com/technology/archive/2011/08/unimate-the-story-of-george-devol-and-the-first-robotic-arm/243716)

Vollmer, Scott. "George Devol—Inventor of the First Industrial Robot." Vimeo. (vimeo.com/23372660; accessed February 9, 2018)

Wallén, Johanna. "The History of the Industrial Robot." *DiVA—Digitala Vetenskapliga Arkivet.* May 8, 2008. (diva-portal.org/smash/get/diva2:316930/FULLTEXT01.pdf)

The Zuckerman Institute at Columbia University. "In witnessing the brain's 'aha!' moment, scientists shed light on biology of consciousness: Study in human participants lends insight into one of neuroscience's greatest puzzles: How the brain transforms unconscious information into conscious thought." ScienceDaily. (sciencedaily.com/releases/2017/07/170727141804.htm; accessed December 19, 2018)

Chapter Nine: Raye Draws Her Own Lines

Adams, Betty Sorensen. "Raye Jean Jordan Montague." *The Encyclopedia of Arkansas History and Culture.* Last modified October 24, 2018. (encyclopediaofarkansas.net/encyclopedia/entry-detail.aspx?entryID=5565)

Chandler, D. L. "Little Known Black History Fact: Raye Montague." Black America Web, February 7, 2017. (blackamericaweb.com/2017/02/07/little-known-black-history-fact-raye-montague)

Collins, Elizabeth. "Breaking Barriers, Part 2." *All Hands*, March 28, 2017. (allhands.navy.mil/Stories/Display-Story/Article/1840330/breaking-barriers-part-2)

Faller, Angelita. "Montague Mother and Son Duo Say Education Is the Key to Breaking Barriers." University of Arkansas. February 24, 2017. (ualr.edu/news/2017/02/24/david-raye-montague-breaking-barriers)

Finley, Taryn. "Janelle Monáe Honors 'Hidden Figure' and Naval Engineer Raye Montague." *Huffington Post*, February 21, 2017. (www.huffingtonpost.com/entry/janelle-monae-hidden-figure-raye-montague_us_58ac50d5e4b0f077b3ee04e7)

Hansan, J. E. "Jim Crow Laws and Racial Segregation." Social Welfare History Project. (socialwelfare.library.vcu.edu/eras/civil-war-reconstruction/jim-crow-laws-andracial-segregation; accessed February 17, 2018)

Johnson, Jajuan S. "Montague, Raye J. Interview." Video. Central Arkansas Library System. January 29, 2009. (cdm15728.contentdm.oclc.org/cdm/ref/collection/p1532coll1/id/12700)

———. "Montague, Raye Jean, Interview." Video. Central Arkansas Library System. February 13, 2009. (cdm15728.contentdm.oclc.org/cdm/ref/collection/p15728coll5/id/871)

Miller, Sharde. "Meet the Woman Who Broke Barriers as a Hidden Figure at the US Navy." ABC News. February 20, 2017. (abcnews.go.com/Entertainment/meet-woman-broke-barriers-hidden-figure-us-navy/story?id=45566924)

Seelye, Katharine Q. "Raye Montague, the Navy's 'Hidden Figure' Ship Designer, Dies at 83." *New York Times,* October 18, 2018. (nytimes.com/2018/10/18/obituaries/raye-montague-a-navy-hidden-figure-ship-designer-dies-at-83.html)

Vicinanzo, Amanda. "'Hidden Figure of US Navy' Raye Montague Speaks at Dahlgren." Fredericksburg.com. April 4, 2017. (www.fredericksburg.com/news/local/king_george/hidden-figure-of-u-s-navy-raye-montague-speaks-at/article_e88759ab-2b49-5d19-8759-91efefb97803.html)

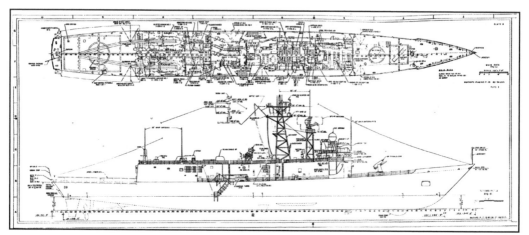

Outboard profile of the US Navy frigate USS *Rodney M. Davis* (FFG-60), United States Navy

Index

1885

Gasoline-powered
motorcycle—
Gottlieb Daimler

1885

Gasoline-powered
automobile—
Karl Benz

1892

Escalator—
Jesse Reno

1893

Ferris wheel—
George Ferris

1898

Drone—
Nikola Tesla

1900

Hybrid car—
*Ferdinand Porsche
and Jacob Lohner*

1903

First successful
documented airplane
flight—
Orville and Wilbur Wright

1903

Windshield wipers—
Mary Anderson

1920

Quadcopter—
Étienne Oehmichen

1925

Interstate bus—
Eric Wickman

1925

Self-driving car—
Francis Houdina

1926

Liquid-fuel-propelled
rocket—
Robert H. Goddard

1930

Jet engine—
Frank Whittle

1933

Folding wheelchair—
*Herbert Everest and
Harry Jennings*

1939

Helicopter—
Igor Sikorsky

1940

Unmanned aerial
vehicle (UAV)—
Edward Sorenson

1949

Flying car—
Moulton Taylor

1957

Satellite—
various creators